HAND IN HAND

by MARY LEE

Tender Bough
Hand in Hand

HAND IN HAND

POEMS AND ILLUSTRATIONS BY MARY LEE

Crown Publishers, Inc. New York

Warm brown body
by me
in the
warm balmy breeze
Perched
in our netted nests
skimming
across
long swaying leaves.

And you, as an angel
dressed in gentle brown skin
covering me with the feathers I need
shining the light through my soul
being godly you're giving
I'm receiving I'm living
the days I remember from paradise past
illusion tells me that this is the last
moment before I die
truth rustles gently
like your hair on my neck
and I know that this is the last
moment before I am born.

He crept in
with his magic key
in the stillness
of the night
and lit a fire
under me
infusing my reality
with embers of delight.

Short stubby grass
chunky and thick beneath our feet.
Sky is almost violet
fiery pink behind a distant hill.
These hills are clumps of clay
unevenly shaped
covered with this dark short grass.

Morning's different
when the ground is moist and soft.
The spongey grass
gives way so easily
hilly slopes
as if they're bending down
fine muscular forms
emerald waves
of movement.

Hand in hand
on a purple night
we walk across
cool crumpled sand
past kelp and broken shells.

Floods of warm moonlight
and spurts of energy
from the stars
roll us lazily
into the swells.

Hand in hand
in the purple chill
we sink into
oblivion
past kelp and swimming shells.

The clouds enclosed me today
in a fine translucent mist
glimmering my thoughts away.
I felt like I'd been kissed
by the morning star
or held for a joyous eternity
within the arms of God.
Then the sun awoke the world
and the sunlight aroused the sky.
A small bird appeared with green feathers
and I touched him with my hand.
I thought he had something to say
but he looked at me as father, as son,
and just smiled and flew away.

Lofty cliffs and oceans gleaming
cloudless skies and sunlight streaming
warm in ecstasy of golden dreaming
opening my self to you as woman
tenderly you enter in as man
joining to create a new dominion
where love and joy are freely sown
and yet I wonder when I'm alone,
where is the fruit of our union?

I fear that we have loved in haste
that what you gave was just a taste
but oh so sweet and long awaited
all other thoughts have been erased.

There within your windowed room
weaving patterns on a loom
of sensual interlacing, warm, elated
pouring life into my womb.

Then the gentle afterlove of sleep
held in the night sky's starry keep
that moment my destiny was fated
so filled with joy it made me weep.

Fears go as quickly as they come.
The hand of God will choose the one
to whom my soul is to be mated,
so how can I regret this thing we've done?

I live my life.
I lace my shoes,
I tie my hair,
I see new views
of the same old situations,
living always in expectation
of that unforeseen occasion,
a lullaby of persuasion
when braids unravel
and bare-skinned we travel
with feet hardly touching the ground.
When we stop to look around
in the vibrance
of the presence
we, in our pure essence,
share a glimpse of celestial freedom.

The constant struggle with submission
is tiring.
This so-called strength I've gained
is just another heavy load.
I wish to curl myself into a fetal rose
and rest in the eternal womb awhile.

Only to be born again refreshed
and welcomed into life again by you.
To be the child of your spirit
until we've grown as one
and lifted from us all the bonds of time
to live eternally forever free.

Lines of scribble on a pad
words exchanged of what we've had
and what we're lacking
all this talk and backtracking
is getting us nowhere

I'm trying to touch you
but I feel that I'm failing
maybe it's just my mind
sailing off in fantasy
but honestly
it's hard to think of love
in any other way than
idealistically
magically
eternally.

She comes like an eclipse
and blights the light we kindled
her black hair streaming, brightness dwindles
as you go with her, your kiss still on my lips
She's my thorn, your mocking goddess,
naked river nymph, daughter of Mars.

A spirit called
Flux
haunts me
the fear
and the chaos
of change
the tomorrow
that can't be defined
the place that can't be named.

Another pair of groping
hands have left me
prodded and probed
trodden exposed
beaten battered
flattened tattered
feathers ruffled
sighs muffled
trudged across me
searched for something
they didn't find
so they've gone
echoing thundering
thumping
like the beats
of my heart.

My love,
if my soliciting should make you moan
and all you wish is to be left alone
then, pray, forgive
but I live
within a state of wandering
my soul is such a seeking thing.
The trees of late have bloomed again
and with them comes your name's refrain
calling up the images of sleep
leading me I know not where, so deep
into my memory have I gone
no more can I distinguish dusk from dawn.
I beseech you once again
to free me from my own disdain
to let me look upon your face
to close the gap that villain space
has laid between us.
I must clear the questions from my heart
and leave unburdened or sadly part
from you as I have done before
this is all I ask, and nothing more.

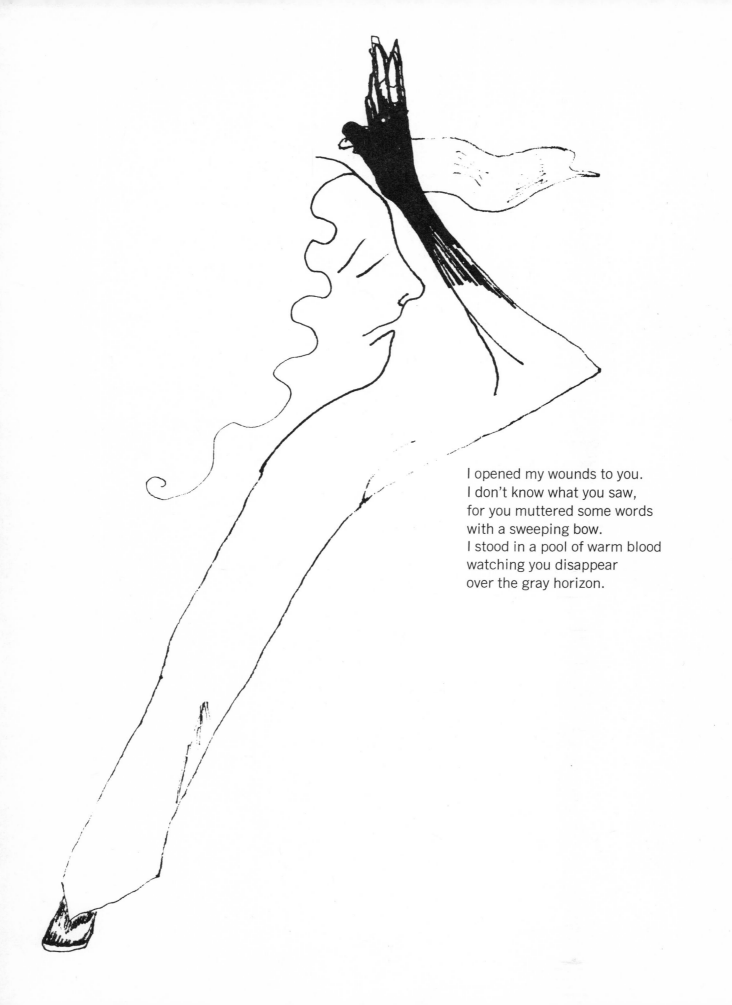

I opened my wounds to you.
I don't know what you saw,
for you muttered some words
with a sweeping bow.
I stood in a pool of warm blood
watching you disappear
over the gray horizon.

I remember words uttered not so long ago
they were gifts I'd waited long to hear
they showed me your sincerity
they made things all so clear
but somewhere between then and now
the words have slipped away
and I can't quite remember
what you meant to say
just the sounds and your
big brown eyes.

My love, I'm scared.
There is no word, no vow
that can assure me now
that you, or you and I, will last
no promise that when you've passed
I will not ache in loneliness.
What is the cause of my unrest?
Lack of faith, uncertainty,
impatience, insecurity.
It is with shame
that I admit my doubt
but only time will see the out-
come.
Only you can calm
my sore distress,
that is unless
I can suspend this need for love.

I feel the emptiness still.
The evening sun creeping
through the open door
draws the last bits of color away.
This wretched hollow loneliness
that wants your arms about me
has seeped in with the twilight
turning everything to gray.

You're fading in my mind
like the bearer of the Ring
an abdicating king
gone so soon,
a slowly waning moon
reflecting weakly
a time that meekly
is retreating.
What remains is but a mist
all our love must have been kissed
away.
So many hours were just wished
away.
But my foresight is returning
gradually I'm learning
to hold but not to grasp
to let the months lapse
into years
to shed my tears
for greater causes.

I lean against the wind.
My eyeless head
is empty,
an abandoned shell
bleached white by time.
Only a speck of sunlight
piercing through the storm
reaches me.
It finds my solitude
intrudes
disrupts
and crushes me
against the sand
in tiny fragments
scattered strewn about.
I think you found a piece of me
when you rose above the dunes
and swept down in
a gust of light.
But I'll never know.
I've lost that moment now.
All I hear is where you've been.
Delayed resonance,
the sad sound of Sunday.

The night tide's
receded
showing
skulls and broken ships,
protruding from
the shining sand.

I remember
Ships and Men.
Sails full
hearts full
coming to me
from the west.
Now they rest
and I stroll the beach
alone.

Clip-clopping wooden heels
scuffling along through miles and miles
of wilderness
wearing holes
through leather soles
tired in the summer sun.

Near far little round animals
gnawing on chunks of wood
scurry beneath the brush
a slaughtered thrush
rotting in the summer sun.

Dust and heat sucking up my eyes
lungs parched and seared
I'm going to die.

God I beg you
lead me to my end
earth I know
you'll lead me to my end.

Soft sloping hills
climbing easily now beyond
the barren wilderness
breathing freer
rising nearer
to the summer sun.

Stopping to remember
a tinge of sadness sighs
a brief relapse
then I collapse
and join the summer sun.

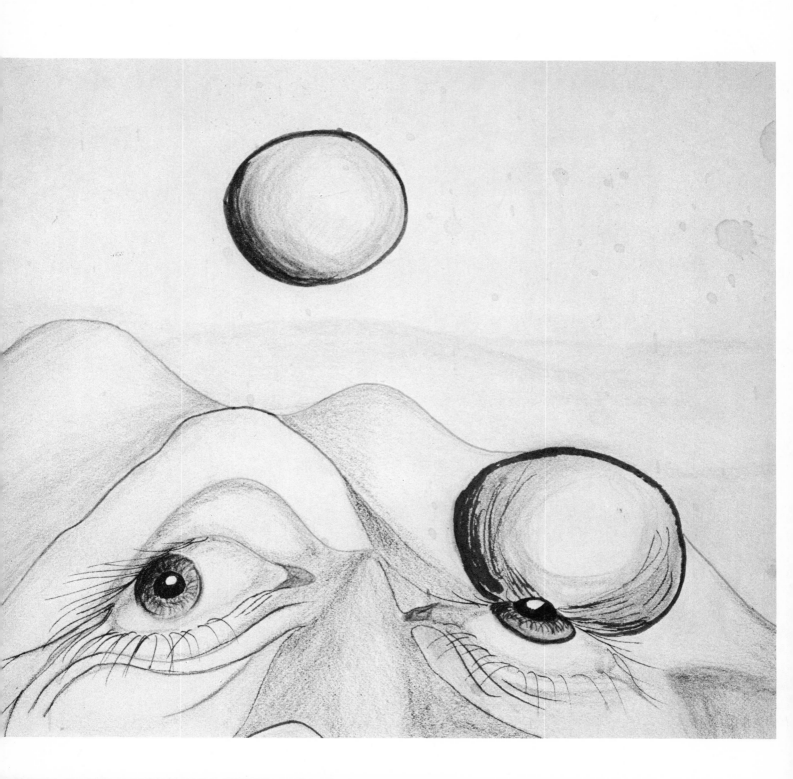

A spider crawled across my eye
I saw him inside out
a giant sprawling thing
He didn't notice me
until I flicked him
down upon the ground
and smashed him with my fist
I watched in horror
as he humbly crumpled
into a tiny falling thing
defeated
then he stopped
and with one last spasm
shot his soul into the wind.

My spirit entombed
mother aries womb
warm fluid peace erupts
from timelessness she thrusts
me towards another death
I gasp a bitter breath

within the walls of childhood
solitude's comfort is good
time dispels illusions
friends passing in confusion
one unfolds my skin
and slips quietly in

I leave the confines of my mind
to journey in the undefined
within the ordered rows of reason
doubts replaced by optimism
valleys draped in greenery
I'm soothed in sweet serenity

Clear music
whirls through
swirling smoke
I hear it
I near it
I pass through
weightlessly
Marranan's
released me
In spirit
I'm warming.

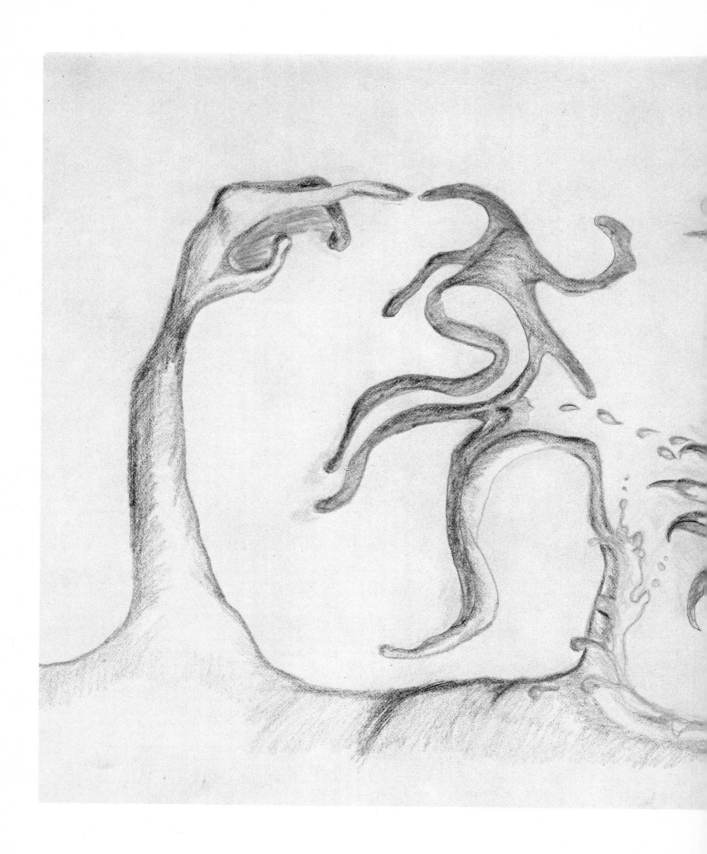

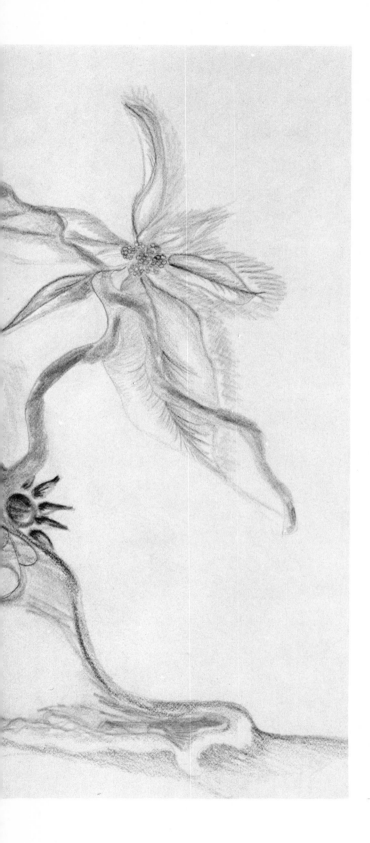

The magic process
Growth
is the divine on earth
The unique gift
to nature
Life.
When God unfolds
and is fulfilled
the shores of time
depart,
life's waters
become One.

Somewhere a soul is floating
weightless in Cosmic Splendor
black as the gates of Mordor
the earth is gloating
beckoning deceitfully
offering selfishly
the "pleasures" of the world

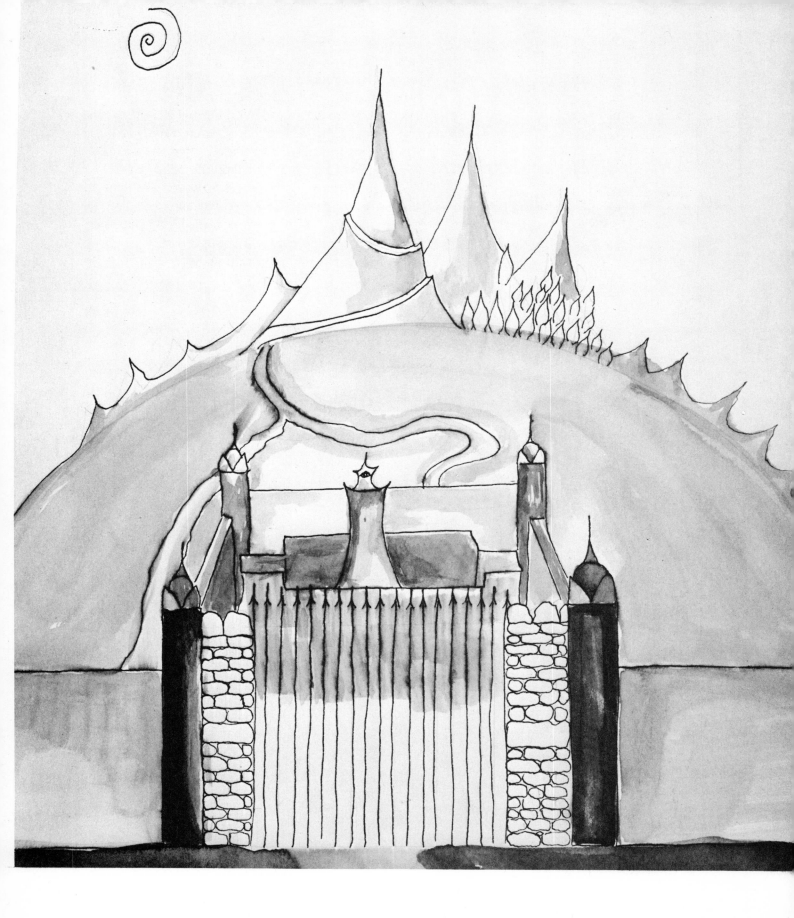

I left on a mission seems ages ago
(as ages go seems no time at all)
Long heavy lashes swept clear my eyes
Churches were waving their children goodbye
Lovers kept clinging and tearing their hair
Blackness surrounded and then cleared the air
In silence a voice rang to beckon the dead
They sent forth their children who were naked instead
And the earth could do nothing but open her jaws
And screaming hordes streamed in without pause
But now they're all gone, no one is left
Except Mother and Father God to clean up the mess.

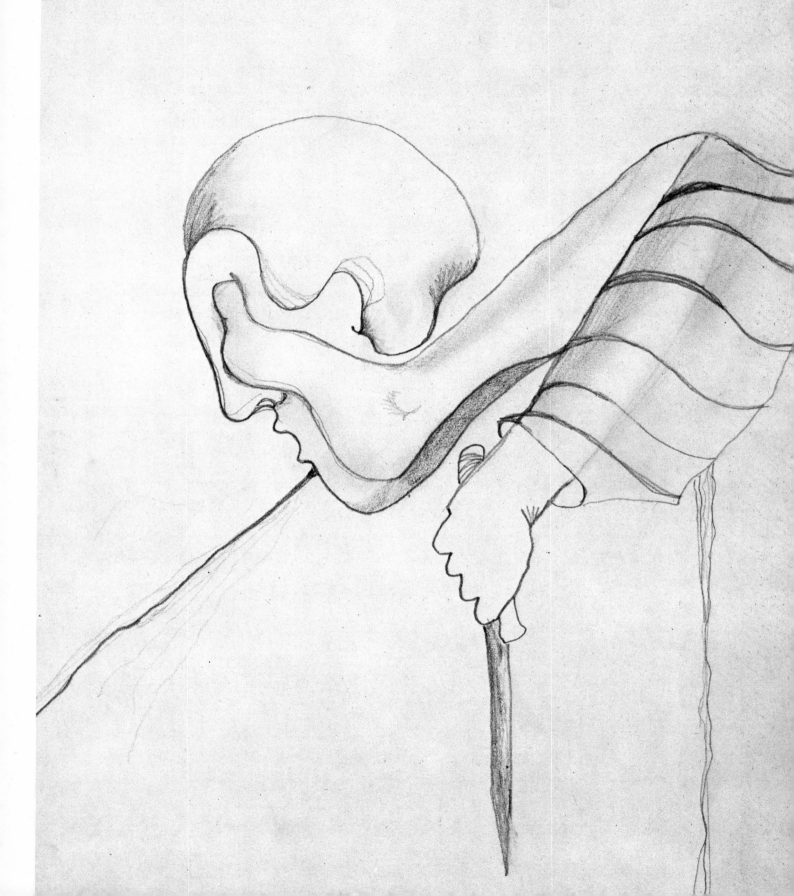

The sunset is receding
behind the hills of Tiburon
and everything is slowing down
and cooling off
A moment's rest
upon this
macrocosmic mobile
in the wind.

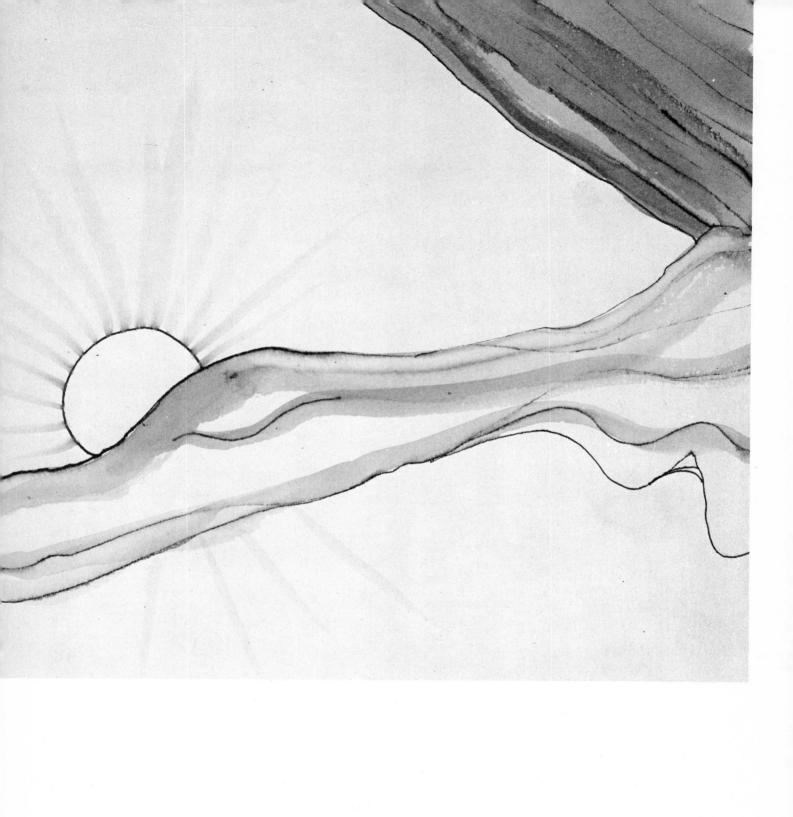

While strolling in a silver glen
as fair as fair Lothlorien
from all around a tale I heard
without a single spoken word.

It told of everlasting peace
rustling with the lacy trees
crystalline splashes of the waters
sang of heaven's long-lost daughters.

Whistling clearly the tingling breeze
heralded the rising of the seas.
The coming age was clearly shown
upon reflecting polished stones.

The song rings still within the glen
for all who shun the ways of men,
for there a prayer of peace is heard
without a single spoken word.

When you were my first and only love
I thought you were my happiness too
I found you weren't
your fire burnt
a hole through the illusion
the first conclusion
formed within my mind
which finally put the past behind
opening up a world
of new concepts and ideals
marveling in the way it feels
to be a wounded woman
my compassion for the lonely grows
I have known
the threat of isolation
helplessness frustration
but my resistance to the fact
is softening
I no longer care to nurture
broken dreams
to view life only as it seems
is the first cause of grief
what relief
when I renew my faith
in the sacred purposes of life.

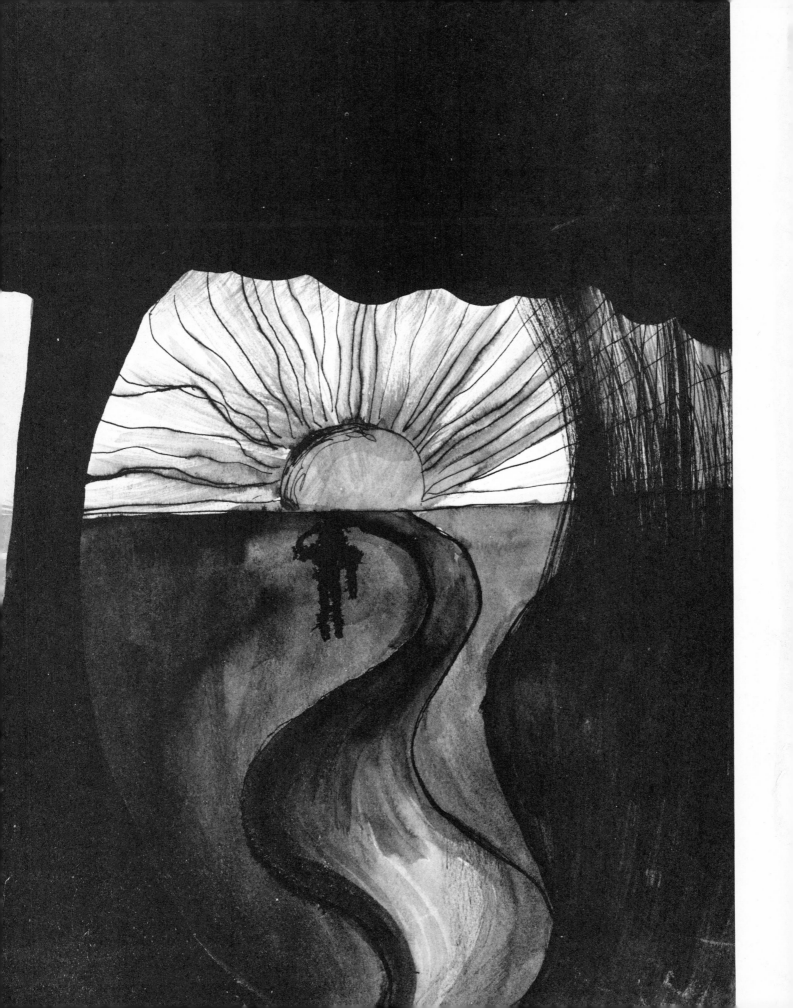

Mithril. A silver thread
invisible
but for moonlight
shining on
its silken sheen.

A silver turn
inaudible
but for silence
opening up
to chiming vines.

Many cherished thoughts
forgotten
but for sensitivity
peeling away mortality.

Eternally revolving round the sun
in monumental circles do we move.
In turn our galaxy in orbit, one
of many ages, comes and goes to prove
a thing or two to unbelieving souls.
The Zodiac reclines across the sky
a guiding line that leads us to our goals,
illuminating every mystery.
The father of Man, as Adam has been named,
first breathed with Taurus, sign of Mother Earth,
and Abraham gave warmth to Aries flame
while Pisces waters burst in Virgin birth.
And now Aquarius approaching fast,
may man receive the light of Holy Mass.

Ancient instincts
aroused
as steaming beams
of hues diffuse
steaming through
orgasmic prisms
enfolding me
in golden visions.

Abortion

Melon head of virgin dreams
wrapped in rainbow dew
tiny teacup hands and feet
nothing harsh will touch you
no, nothing, nothing at all
and you won't really mind will you
since you're still so small.

No cries need be uttered, baby
no tears be ever shed
I wonder if life's misery
will ever reach the dead.
I don't know, and I'll never hear
the answer come from you
so sleep on, baby, close your eyes
and sleep gently right on through.

There's no one to write home to
we've brought them all along
just the echoes and the patterns
of the shadows on the lawn
it's a little cold for winter
and yet it's almost spring
the blankets need a pressing
and a thought that needs expressing
soon dries up and leaves no vapors
like a hollow honeycomb.

Changing my mind
Changing my name
Everything seems different
but it's still all the same
Losing my mind
losing my gains
I may have lost everything
and yet so much remains
which is noticed for the first time
recognized like coming out of sleep
emerging from a hollow deep
in a wordless pantomime
Thanking the stars
Thanking the night
strange as it seems
I know all is right.

I was thirsty so I drank
from a clear blue stream.
I was filled with sleep
and laid my tired soul upon the wind.
Eager to explore the passages
within my heart, the unknown
an inner light shone forth
I stood stiff-kneed before my pasts
and blinked as memory flashed
a whirling dance.
I saw you many times
unrecognized in face.
Your velvet eyes remained the same
and pierced me with a tender pain.

I saw the struggle in your eyes
your face laid bare your sorrow.
I knew how ominous tomorrow
seemed, a giant with eyes
luminous, all seeing.
And I knew that if I took your hand
you'd never turn to see
the magic land within yourself,
so I focused my attention there
and you looked upon the ground
seeing only shadows of the truth.
You didn't hear the sounds
you didn't see the life
within your soul.

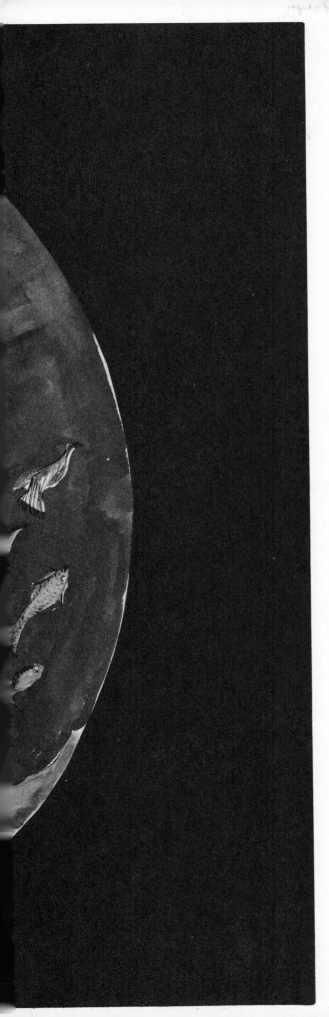

The floor just split
and I'm free falling
a million miles per second.
Flicks of color bouncing
off the walls,
the far cornered walls
of my mind.
And they're crumbling
crashing silently into the void.
I can only surrender myself
and submit to the waves of rebirth.

The flat gray sea is slowly turning blue
We greet the sunrise lying intertwined
A coolness like the blueness
of the air
                    I feel
as if you were not real
I love you as I love the sea
distantly and passively
I'm drawn to you but do not yield
I am a creature of the land
The moments that I spend
removed, immersed in loving you
are isolated thought dreams shared
They bloom and burst
like waves against the cliffs
I only want your gentleness
to leave me shimmering in the sunrise.

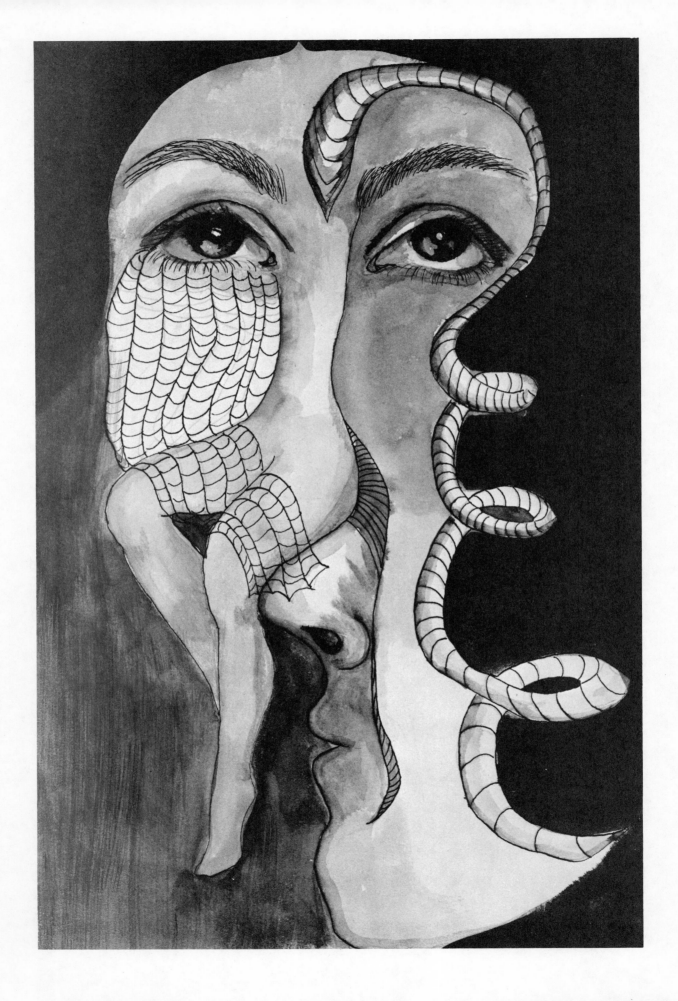

Words like tired dewdrops
fall heavily from my lips
embrace the lifeless space
and form a web of wonder,
can these thoughts be mine?
Somewhere in the blackness
I am answered.
His eyes extend in gracefulness
and strength, uplifting cleansing.
Beyond the world of words
I find myself.
Another cycle ends.
The spiral cycle of life.

I sleep for a time
in a small little ball
at the base of it all
until I'm awakened
drawn like a flower
upwards unfolding
shining and growing.
Love is our being
we've escaped time and space
revolving on realities' peaks
galaxies lighted
duality united
love's being is multiple
and we are its being.

I came from a star
my mind was an island
someone was speaking
in a place near a river
eyes were exploding
like organic mushrooms
causing temptation
to forfeit his chances
to dive in the river
to wash away swiftly
and never be found.
But that's not why I'm with you
we're not on an island
the lesson to master
is who is the pupil
and whose hazy pupils
see all of the truth.

Not in sleep
have I dreamed
a dream so deep
and dear.
Not a thought
could have brought
me such peace
such ease
nor release
so blissful,
this kiss full
of nectar
to my thirsting lips.
Within my ringing
ears I hear
a paean peeling
reeling clear
"enjoy, enjoy."

I put them all away
those tangled troubled thoughts
opened all the portals wide
turned it all around, inside out
feeling good enough to shout
loud and clear into the air
that now revitalizes me, my hair
is full of life and dancing.
Oh these moments movements
smiles and sighs
at last I finally realize
as long as we release the past
and live each moment as our first
timeless love will always last
so solid steady sound and fast.

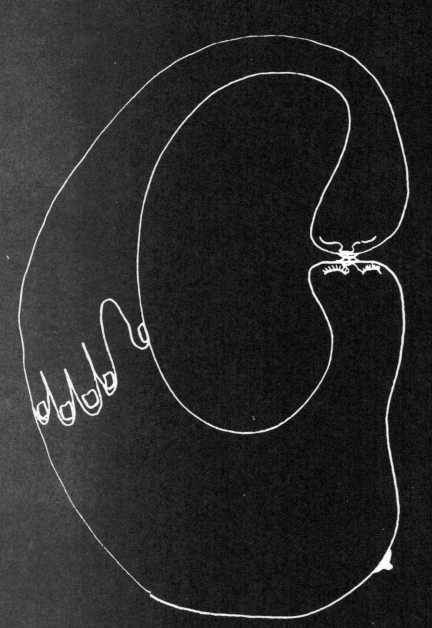

I love you
I desire you
and oh
I long to soothe you
to calm you
to caress you
and then
to gently smooth you
trust me
I mean it
you know
you've seen it
my soul, my spirit
you've come so near it
take it don't fear it
there's so much to gain
this sorrow and pain
is only the rain
washing clear what remains
of slow-to-go stains
but love overcomes
when two become one
I'll bear half your burdens
I'll bear you a son
we've born such fine happiness
that can't be undone
trust me
I mean it
you know
you've seen it.

My reasoning means nothing
all qualifying is absurd
you are the love of my life
the magic echoing word.

Here within this numbly nimbus state
rolling slowly through the gate
down the hill past the lake
to you where you await

catching you within my private cloud
softening the sounds that drone so loud
they tinkle like water dripping now

Shedding our town and soiled shrouds
standing free unbound, joyous, proud
in the light of the union we've avowed
Children of the future living now
eager to fulfill the laws of love.

Embryos of heritage divine
leaving our hermitage behind
witnessing the marriages of Time
and Eternity, they chime
so musically and intertwine
The melody and harmony
of life's mystery itself
unveiled before our eyes.